THE MOON AND THE WEATHER

BY

JOHN WESTWOOD OLIVER

ISBN-13:
978-1727076684

ISBN-10:
1727076680

THE persistent survival of weather-lore in these days of intellectual emancipation is not at all remarkable when we consider the extent to which the vulgar sayings embody real truths. A few years ago Messrs. Abercromby and Marriott embarked on an extremely interesting inquiry with a view to determine, by actual comparison, how far the popular proverbs express relations, or sequences, which the results of meteorological science show to be real. The investigation proved that something like a hundred of the more popular sayings are, under ordinary conditions, trustworthy. Such being the case, we need not be surprised that simple country folk prefer familiar couplets to all the "isobars," "cyclones," and "synchronous charts," in the world. If "hills clear, rain near," means the same as "the presence of a wedge-shaped area of high pressure, accompanied by great atmospheric visibility, is likely to be followed by the advance of a disturbance with rain and southerly winds," which for all practical purposes it does, the preference is justified on the mere ground of breath economy. The thirty-one words demanded by science stand no chance against four.

But it is unfortunate that, along with the limited number of folk-sayings founded on truth, there has survived, a very large number founded on the grossest error. These latter have borrowed credence and respect from the proved credibility of the others, and apparently they are all destined to sink or swim together. Hammer as we will at certain favorite proverbs which we know to be based upon error, it is all in vain. The reverence for tradition is too much for us. And of all the superstitions, pure and simple, which defy our attempts at destruction, the most invulnerable are those ascribing certain effects to the influence of the moon. Few of the counties in England, Scotland, and Ireland but have their own peculiar observances referring to the supposed lunar influence upon diseases, destiny, etc. To merely enumerate these would require a small volume. Any who may care to see some specimens should consult a curious collection (but far from an exhaustive one) published last year by the Rev. Timothy Harley, under the title "Moon Lore." And of equal vitality with the other moon-myths is the idea of lunar influence upon the weather. There is this important difference, however, that while the attribution* of supernatural powers to the moon is palpably and admittedly absurd, the idea of her influence on the weather is not founded on anything physically impossible, and has the sanction of striking analogy in the accepted doctrine of the tides. How much importance was attached to the inquiry, regarded as a true scientific investigation, in the earlier half of the century, and up even to very recent years, may be seen by consulting a meteorological bibliography. The constant succession of papers in English, French, and German, by accredited scientific men, and contributed to respectable scientific societies and periodicals, dealing with the lunar weather theory in all its aspects, shows this to have been long considered one of the most important problems of meteorology.

The doctrine of the survival of the fittest would not seem to be applicable to the case of wise saws. The criterion of fitness we may take to be the reliableness of the saw, and, as we have just seen, they survive without the slightest reference to that characteristic. Nevertheless, one is loath to believe that formulated nonsense can have found credence for ages unless there is a larger admixture of truth in it than is readily apparent by the light of our present knowledge. Popular error has been described as the perception of half the truth, or of one side of a truth. "Were this invariably so, it would afford a profitable employment to dissect popular errors with a view to discovering the half-truth, since we might be able to find its complement somewhere, and materially enrich the world. But that is not the sense I intend to convey. Nearly all weather sayings are of the nature of predictions. They describe a certain appearance of phenomenon, and then go on to say what other appearance or phenomenon may be expected to follow it. We have here a sequence of events; the ground of the saying (if it has any ground at all) is the invariability of the sequence. Now it is difficult to imagine such sequences being invented without any reference to the observed fact, and it is still more difficult to imagine them obtaining currency—not local currency merely, but sometimes universal currency—unless a certain number of observed instances have borne them out. Of course, by the laws of chances any sequence within the range of probability is bound to happen sometimes, but a sequence of weather phenomena is liable to variation in so many different directions that the purely chance happenings of any specified sequence are not numerous relatively to the blanks. I am disposed to assume, therefore, that all weather proverbs of this nature are founded upon one observed instance; and that, although many are only based upon the accidental recurrence of the sequence (and are consequently worthless), many also are the expression of a real, demonstrable sequence of sufficiently frequent occurrence to afford ground for the rough approximation which suffices to constitute a popular weather law.

But it does not follow that because we assume the fact of an apparent connection between two phenomena, and predict from the manifestation of the one the approaching manifestation of the other, the connection must necessarily be of the nature of cause and effect, nor yet of the nature of successive effects of the same cause. There is such a thing as the coincidence of phenomena. The coincidence may be purely fortuitous, or it may be the result of the operation of higher laws of which we as yet have no knowledge.

We may now proceed to the more immediate subject of this article. It is not my intention to attempt to give an exhaustive collection of lunar proverbs. Such collections are curious, but they are not particularly useful. Nor do I aspire to propound any new theory of lunar influence on the weather. What I do propose is to discuss a few of the best known, and therefore most important, of the popular weather notions in which the moon is concerned, with the view of showing the necessity for discrimination in their acceptance; the ultra-scientific man who pooh-poohs everything that has moon in it being really as wide of the mark as the poor victim of superstition who puts double faith in things on the same ground. In arranging my remarks it will be convenient to deal successively with (1) lunar notions that are utterly absurd; and (2) those that are explicable by the aid of physical principles, and are therefore rational and useful in practice.

To the former class belongs the idea, in its various forms, of a direct lunar influence; and I would begin with that most ubiquitous—and apparently everlasting as well—of all popular absurdities, the table known as "Herschel's Weather Table." How it ever came to be associated with the name of the greatest of English astronomers is a mystery. I once put the question in "Notes and Queries," where the obscurest of literary enigmas are often solved, but to no purpose. Whatever the explanation may be, the table is certainly weighted with Herschel's great authority, and to this day we find it in nearly all the almanacs, and even in some less ephemeral publications, gravely quoted as the embodiment of scientific truth. It is not necessary to take up space with the whole table, as it is only too well known, and can be seen in almost any almanac. It states that if the moon changes, or becomes full, or enters her first or third quarter between noon and two in the afternoon, the "resulting weather" (that is, I presume, the weather during the ensuing week, or until a new change inaugurates a new state of things) will be, in summer, "very rainy," and in winter "snow and rain." If the change of moon takes place between two and four in the afternoon, the resulting weather will be "changeable" in summer (a pretty safe prediction in this climate), and "fair and mild" in winter. And so on for the whole twenty-four hours. Now, it will be observed that the lunar influence assumed here is of an occult nature. There is no pretense of physical agency in the matter. The weather will be such and such, not because the moon's reflection of light is greater or smaller, nor because her radiation of heat is more or less, nor because her position with respect to the earth is nearer or farther away, but simply because she "changes" between certain arbitrary hours. What virtue there can be in the moon's "change" is hard indeed to see. The principle involved must be an astrological one, for in reality the moon is gradually, if imperceptibly, "changing" during every moment of her increase from new to full, and her decrease from full to new again, the quarters being only stages in the process specially marked for the sake of convenience. There is precisely the same degree of visible difference between a three-days'-old moon and a ten-days'-old one as there is between a new moon and a moon in her first quarter; but in the former case (so we are asked to believe) the difference is impotent to rule the weather because it does not coincide with the conventional "change." To look at the matter in another way, it will be noticed that the table provides for a change occurring at any hour in the twenty-four, and, as the moon can not escape the necessity of changing sometimes, it follows that the weather for the year—and not only for the year, but for as long as the sun, earth, and moon retain their relative position and motions—is reducible to a cut-and-dry order; such an order, no doubt, as the compilers of Zadkiel's, Orion's, and the Belfast Almanacs assume. Need the British public be assured that no such convenient orderliness in our weather phenomena exists? And, finally, the "changes" of the moon are not exclusively confined to

England, nor to any one country. The new moon waxes into the full moon simultaneously all the world over. Moreover, the "change" takes place simultaneously all the world over. Consequently, when the change occurs between 12 and 2 P. M., it means that the weather will be "very rainy" in every part of the earth where summer is, while "snow" must prevail wherever the conditions are such as to make rain impossible; and what becomes of those local variations which are the experiences of everybody who has traveled twenty miles upon the terrestrial globe? Predictions founded upon this preposterous weather table are not one whit more worthy of serious attention than those contained in Zadkiel's Almanac; but, while the latter are admittedly addressed only to the grossly ignorant and credulous, the table unfortunately retains its character of respectability unimpaired.

As an example of elaborate nonsense, I know of nothing better than a table "showing the probabilities of a change of weather at or after each of the moon's situations throughout an entire revolution in her orbit," which received the honor of recognition and approval in a cyclopædia of not very ancient date. The table names the moon's ten "situations "(conjunction, opposition, first quarter, third quarter, perigee, apogee, ascending equinox, descending equinox, northern lunistice, and southern lunistice), and opposite each gives the "chances that the weather will change" with the most exquisite exactitude. Thus, there are six chances to one that a change will take place about new moon, but only five to two in favor of a change about the full. At the time of the northern lunistice the chances are eleven to four, at the southern three to one (note the minute difference). Unlike Herschel's table, this one has reference to a lunar "influence" which depends for its intensity, as any physical influence necessarily would do, upon the nearness or distance of its source, and also upon the position of that source relative to the sun, which may be regarded as the seat of an opposing or antagonistic influence. This is all quite rational, and is well calculated to impress the unscientific mind, while the exquisite precision with which the probabilities are stated, greatly enhances the effect. But what is the outcome of it? Taking the ten specified points in each lunation, and calling a lunation, roughly, thirty days, and then averaging the "probabilities," we discover that this table, which looks for all the world as if it might be the condensed result of years of observation and much laborious calculation, merely expresses (or, more properly speaking, conceals) the simple fact, that in every three days there are about three chances to one that the weather will undergo a change!—which, so far as this country is concerned, is only too true.

"If Christmas comes during a waxing moon we shall have a very good year; and the nearer to the new moon the better. But if, during the waning moon, a hard year; and the nearer the end of the moon, so much the worse." This saying is typical of a good many others. The fact that a festival is invariably selected, points to a purely superstitious origin, for we have no physical grounds for supposing a festival-day to determine the weather conditions which are to follow any more than an ordinary day. Unlike the tables we have been discussing, there is not even the semblance of scientific authority here. The chief agent is not physical, but religious. The moon is always either waxing or waning; it is her nature so to do. But that of itself signifies nothing; it is when Christmas happens upon a waxing or waning period that we have the critical combination.

Southey, in one of his letters, writes: "Poor Littledale has this day explained the cause of our late rains, which have prevailed for the last six weeks, by a theory which will probably be as new to you as it is to me. 'I have observed,' he says, 'that when the moon is turned upward, we have fine weather after it; but if it is turned down, then we have a wet season: and the reason, I think, is, that when it is turned down it holds no water, like a basin, you know, and then down it all comes.'" Southey found, upon inquiry, that this was a common notion in the lake district. George Eliot, as Mr. Harley points out, has a reference to the same fancy in "Adam Bede." If Jamieson's "Scottish Dictionary" is to be trusted, the same belief is exactly reversed in Scotland. Jamieson states that it is considered as an almost infallible presage of *bad* weather if the moon "lies sair on her back." Of the two forms of the saying, the English one is infinitely to be preferred, for it embodies rather a pretty idea, while the Scotch one is simply nonsensical. The moon might "lie sair on her back" were it she herself that was "bad," but scarcely on account of an approaching disturbance of the weather. To explain the conditions under which the crescent moon is tilted forward or backward, would require little short of a treatise on the lunar, and terrestrial motions, a digression for which we have no space; but it is sufficiently obvious that to attribute an influence to the "attitude" of the visible moon is open to the fatal objection that, like the "change," it is not a sudden but a gradual phenomenon, which ought to exercise its influence through all the stages of its progress, instead of only when a weather-wise person happens to notice it.

One of the most curious, and certainly one of the most widespread, of all weather beliefs is that of the "Saturday moon." The notion is that when the new moon falls on a Saturday it is invariably followed by a period of wet and unsettled weather. The currency of this belief is remarkably wide. Not only is it found (more or less modified) in the folk-lore of England, Scotland, and Ireland, but it is held also by seamen of all nationalities. A traveler relates that he once heard it referred to by a Chinese pilot. And more than this, in 1848, a Dr. Forster announced to the Royal Astronomical Society, as the result of an examination of weather registers kept by his grandfather, his father, and himself, extending over nearly eighty years, that nineteen times out of twenty a new moon on Saturday was followed by twenty days of rain and wind. It is not many weather sayings that enjoy the supporting testimony of a sober scientific investigation, and that circumstance, together with the general acceptance in which the saying is held, entitles it to special consideration.

Could we reduce the occurence of a Saturday moon to any form of periodicity—that is to say, were the accident of the new moon falling on a Saturday to recur at regular intervals—we should have some ground for at least provisionally admitting the truth of the rule, since we know that many weather phenomena are roughly periodical (though the periodicity is often completely masked by the disturbing operation of local influences), and it might so happen that this weather period coincided with that of the Saturday moon. The "cold snaps" in May» for example, recur periodically; and a cause for the phenomenon has been found in the passage of dense meteor flights between the sun and the earth, the meteors intercepting a portion of his heat. But the Saturday moon is not exactly periodical. In 1881 not a single new moon fell on a Saturday. In 1883 there were three conjunctions so distinguished. This year there are two. What sort of weather period can we imagine guilty of such eccentricities? Of course, had the adage referred to a particular Saturday moon it would have been different. The new moon falls on the same day again after a lapse of about nineteen years (a circumstance that gave rise to the Metonic cycle), and the rule would then have meant that a period of wet and windy weather occurred at a certain season every nineteen years—a notion in striking accordance with a favorite cycle of the cycle hunters. No such interpretation is possible, however, and we are obliged to include this much-respected saying in the category of idle superstitions.

We come now to the more edifying class of lunar weather notions—those that have a real physical basis. And it may not be out of place to repeat here that the writers who so emphatically and unreservedly denounce the moon and weather idea a vulgar superstition overstep the limits of scientific truth. So far as any influence of the kind we have been considering is concerned, they are quite right. The moon exerts no influence upon our atmosphere strong enough, by comparison with the other influences at work, to produce a marked correspondence between the lunar and atmospheric phenomena. Of that we are certain. Let us, therefore, belabor the false doctrine upon which the preceding and many similar notions are founded with all our might. But because the moon certainly is not a dominant factor in our weather, it does not follow that we are justified in denying to it an influence of any kind. And the results of sundry investigations have been such as to render it prudent to regard the existence of *some* physical connection between the two as at least an open question. Atmospheric tides, due to the moon's attraction, must exist, unless the whole theory of gravitation be wrong, and in a few cases they have been successfully traced in the barometrical records; but in general they are totally obliterated by the ordinary and very much larger disturbances due to other causes. The heating effect of the moon's rays has been the subject of several careful experiments. Melloni, in 1846, started the investigation, and since then Piazzi Smyth (on Teneriffe) and Lord Rosse (at Parsonstown) have endeavored to make precise determinations, with results that place beyond doubt the fact that moonlight does contain a minute proportion of heat-rays, mostly of the dark sort. More recently. Professor Langley's experiments with the bolometer have confirmed that conclusion. In the face of such results, insignificant though they admittedly are by comparison with the effects popularly attributed to lunar influence, it is not correct to say that science absolutely discountenances the notion of any connection between the moon and the weather. For although a barometrical fluctuation so slight as to defy most efforts to discover it, and a thermometrical effect so infinitesimal as to require a very elaborate as well as delicate apparatus to detect it, cannot in any sense be called "weather," it is not unfair to assume—granted the physical influence—that it may work upon the atmosphere in ways to which our instrumental results afford no clew.

We have an example of this in the circumstance which no less careful an observer than Sir John Herschel remarked, "without any knowledge of such a tendency having been observed by others"—the circumstance that the sky is clearer, generally speaking, about the time of full moon than when she is in her quarters. Humboldt mentions this as a fact well known to the pilots and seamen of Spanish America. The explanation has been suggested that clear nights are more *conspicuous* when the moon is full than when the stars alone diffuse their feeble glimmer, and that clearness in the one case is likely to arrest the attention and be remembered more readily than in the other. One might be disposed to accept the explanation did not Herschel plainly state the tendency to disappearance of clouds under the full moon as a meteorological fact; and he was too experienced an observer to be easily misled by an illusion of the memory. Now, both Lord Rosse's experiments with the three-foot mirror, and those of Professor Langley with the bolometer, have proved that the lunar heat-rays are chiefly dark rays; and Tyndall has shown that "dark heat" is very ready to undergo absorption. It may, therefore, be inferred that much of the heat sent to us by the moon—the quantity of which varies with her phase—is absorbed by the aqueous vapor in the higher regions of the atmosphere; and the direct result of this must be to raise the temperature of the air above the clouds, cause increased evaporation from their surface, and so effect, in a certain measure, their dispersion. Again, a necessary consequence of the dispersion of the clouds is increased radiation from the earth's surface, producing a reduction of temperature in the air near the ground; and Mr. Park Harrison, who discussed a series of temperature observations made at Oxford, Greenwich, and Berlin, found a mean decrease of more than 2° F. about the time of full moon. The French proverb of *la lune rousse,* which Louis XVIII bewildered Laplace by asking him to explain, may be accounted for by the aid of these researches. The name of "red moon" is applied to the moon which is full at the end of April or early in May, because during the clear nights which then prevail, the tender leaves and buds are frozen and turn red; and popular superstition attributes this effect to the peculiar action of the "red moon's" rays. It is at least curious that the connection assumed in this superstition between the full moon, clear nights, and May frosts should be one that is suggested by independent scientific results.

Apart from any question of lunar influences, however, there are many popular prognostics which make use of the moon merely as a convenient exhibitor of certain atmospheric effects—effects which would not be visible without the moon to show them up, but in the production of which that orb plays no part whatever; and in so far as sweeping denunciations of lunar weather proverbs include these, discredit is thrown on a class of useful sayings very unjustly.

There is, perhaps, no better known lunar prognostic than that referred to in the old Scotch ballad of Sir Patrick Spens:

"O ever alack! my master dear,
 I fear a deadly storm.
I saw the new moon late yestreen,
 Wi' the auld moon in her arm;
And if ye gang to sea, maister,
 I fear will suffer harm."

Chambers, in "The Book of Days," says that to see "the old moon in the arms of the new one" is reckoned a sign of *fine* weather—another curious example of how sayings get twisted; but in that statement he is quite wrong. The appearance is almost universally held, to be a sign of bad weather. Two explanations have been offered to account for the prognostic, in each of which there is undoubtedly a measure of truth. When the moon appears "new" to us, the earth would appear "full" to the lunar inhabitants, if there were any; and what causes the dark part of the young moon to be dimly visible is its reflection of the brilliant earth-shine. The earth, however, will not always shine with equal brilliance, even when the same amount of surface is illuminated, for obviously clouds reflect more light than either land or sea. Hence, when an unusual illumination of the night-side of the moon is apparent, it shows that the earth-shine is exceptionally strong, which in turn is an indication of the presence of a large amount of cloud in our atmosphere. Further, as a moment's consideration will prove, the cloud area must lie to the west of us, the direction from which we receive most of our storms; so that the apparition of the old moon in the arms of the new, virtually means that there are vast cloud-banks over the North Atlantic Ocean which, in all probability, are drifting up to us, and will, before long, bring us "dirty" weather. I am not disposed to go so far as Mr. John Aitken, who, in a paper recently read before the Royal Society of Edinburgh, suggested the use of the moon's dark limb as an "outlying signal station," but it is satisfactory to know that this venerable prognostic has a sound physical basis, and is as worthy of respect as ever it was. The other explanation to which I referred is the greater "visibility" of the air which generally precedes rough or unsettled weather, this clearness allowing the ghostly disk of the old moon to loom forth in a way it could not do through a misty atmosphere. Though, doubtless, a part explanation of the phenomenon, it is not a whole one, and must be taken along with the other.

The halo is an old sign of bad weather;

"When round the moon there is a brugh,
The weather will be cold and rough."

Of sixty-one lunar halos observed in the neighborhood of London, thirty-four were followed by rain within twenty-four hours, nineteen by rain within four days, and only eight by no rain at all. The cause of halos is the formation of an extremely attenuated form of cloud which floats in the van of all cyclonic disturbances, Messrs. Abercromby and Marriott, who made a detailed comparison between a number of popular weather prognostics and the actual distribution of weather as disclosed by synoptic charts, found the lunar halo to be a true sign of the approach of a "cyclone" or area of depression, just aa a clear moon indicates the presence of an anti-cyclone, or area of high pressure, with the likelihood of cold or frost. Similarly, a pale or watery moon marks the advent of a disturbance, while the blunting of the cusps is due to the same cause, and has the same significance. The variation of this last prognostic, which makes a sullied lower horn the sign of foul weather before the full, and a sullied upper horn the sign of foul weather about the wane, is purely fanciful.

Just one word about that enticing object of research—as fascinating in its way as perpetual motion or the exact value of π—the lunar circle.

Dr. E. B. Tylor, says: "The notion that the weather changes with the moon's quarterings is still held with great vigor in England. That educated people to whom exact weather records are accessible should still find satisfaction in the fanciful lunar rule, is an interesting case of intellectual survival." I am willing to be with the foremost in combating such absurdities as "Herschel's Weather Table," and all theories which would assign to the lunar phases an immediate control of our weather; but it so happens that the notion Dr. Tylor condemns is one for which there may be some foundation. A moon's quarter is roughly equivalent to a week, and Mr. Carpmael, the Director of the Canadian Meteorological Department, once told me that be had very frequently noticed a tendency in the weather to change and repeat itself every seven days. A similar seven-day periodicity has been observed in the United States. The meteorological conditions of a large continent, it must be remembered, are simpler than those of our own little islands, and hence it is possible that a cycle almost completely masked here might disclose itself there. It is not to be supposed that I am contending for a cycle due to the moon. I only wish to point out that there is some evidence of the existence of a seven-day weather period, which may sometimes happen to be coincident with the lunar phases; and if this be really so, it is not at all wonderful that our forefathers were led to infer a connection, or that even "educated people" continue to put a certain amount of faith in a rule so well founded.

But pre-eminently *the* lunar cycle is that of eighteen and a half years—the ancient Saros, or period of revolution of the lunar node. It has been traced in sundry phenomena, including the amount of rainfall and the recurrence of epidemic pestilences. The evidence, of course, is extremely shaky, though scarcely more so than much of that adduced in favor of the sun-spot cycle. The truth seems to be that in certain lines of inquiry, if an investigator starts with a predetermined system of any kind, statistics will bear him out, or can be made to bear him out.

In closing this hasty survey of a branch of mixed knowledge and ignorance, science combined with superstition, I would repeat the observation with which I set out (and which I have now in a measure justified), that it is unfair to stigmatize the whole moon-and-the-weather theme as unworthy of serious treatment—as a mere surviving fragment of astrology. There is a great deal of nonsense in it, more nonsense than sense; and if the two must sink or swim together, it would be better to let the sense go than to preserve both. But why should they be inseparable? We have sifted a little grain out of much chaff before now; and there is this great gain in the result, that the sifted chaff is chaff, obviously, demonstrably, and can not lay claim to a spurious value in the eyes of the short-sighted by the admixture of a proportion of the valued thing. There are weather wiseacres who *know* that there is truth in some of their cherished lunar proverbs; and the unconditional repudiation of every saying with moon in it by men of science simply convinces these old fellows that the men of science do not understand what they are talking about, and makes them cling all the more vigorously to their ill-used beliefs. If we were to set about it in a different way, and to accept the sayings that science can sanction, and only repudiate the rest, we would have a better chance of success in combating this irrepressible error.

For it is the truth in the error that makes it irrepressible.—*Longman's Magazine.*

Printed in Great Britain
by Amazon